World Book Day

WORLD BOOK DAY'S mission is to offer every child and young person the opportunity to read and love books by giving you the chance to have a book of your own.

To find out more, and for loads of fun activities and recommendations to help you keep reading, visit **worldbookday.com**.

WORLD BOOK DAY is a charity funded by publishers and booksellers in the UK and Ireland.

WORLD BOOK DAY is also made possible by generous sponsorship from National Book Tokens and support from authors and illustrators.

contents

6 It's in your hands

8 We have the power

10 A perfect system

12 The human problem

14 Sustainability

16 Listen up

18 Climate change

20 Switch it off

22 Plant a tree

24 Amazon Rainforest

26 People

28 Conserve water

30 Fast fashion

32 Buying with kindness

34 The Rs

36 What a waste

38 Plastic is not fantastic

40 Ocean plastic

42 Oceans

44 Food

46 Love local

48 Save the bees

50 Protect your patch

52 Endangered species

54 Slow down

56 Have your say

58 Heal the Earth

60 Building for the future

62 Protect the planet

64 Glossary

66 Index

Jess French

is a nature lover who is passionate about protecting the environment. When she's not helping animals as a vet, she's busy writing books to tackle issues that affect them in the wild, such as plastic waste. Her TV work has included presenting the kids' show "Minibeast Adventure with Jess".

Aleesha Nandhra

is an illustrator and printmaker from London. She likes making art that explores themes such as nature, mental health, and music.

Humans are remarkable. They have used their brilliant brains to achieve lots of fantastic things. But humans can also be destructive. Sometimes they forget that the planet is filled with lots of other amazing plants and animals, and they treat it in a way that is not very kind.

Luckily, humans also have the power to reverse some of the bad things they have done. It is not too late to heal the Earth and make it a wonderful place to live for people, plants, and animals.

You may only be small, but you are an incredible human too. That means that YOU have the power to protect the planet, and I'm here to show you how.

I hope this book will plant seeds of ideas, which you can cultivate and develop into a plan of action for saving the Earth. I believe in you and I know that, together, we can make a difference.

Thank you, Earth warriors, and good luck!

Jess

our problem, our responsibility

Lots of the problems faced by the planet are created by humans. But humans also have the power to fix them.

Teamwork makes the dream work

Things are easier to achieve when lots of people work towards the same goal. Join an eco club, attend a march, or connect with young people across the world. It's incredible what we can achieve when we all work together.

We have the power

It can be hard to believe that the individual decisions that we make in our day-to-day lives can make a difference to the planet, but they can. If enough people make choices that are positive for people and the planet, then big changes will follow.

We have the power. We are the solution.

What's your superpower?

You might be an amazing artist or a brilliant writer, an incredible musician or a super sportsperson. Whatever your skills are, use them to make a difference. Draw a picture, write a piece of music, write a blog, or organise a charity sports match. Make your action personal to you.

our planet, our future

We need a healthy planet so that we can live healthy lives. When we work to protect our planet, we protect our futures too.

Kindness is key

By acting in a way that is kind to plants, animals, the environment, and other people, we have the power to save our planet.

A perfect system

The Earth controls temperature, soil, oceans, and gases to provide ideal conditions for all living things. Every animal and plant has a role to play in this system. When everything goes to plan, it runs perfectly.

Terrific trees

Trees take in harmful carbon dioxide and produce oxygen. They also hold soil in place and provide homes for many plants and animals.

Recycling resources

Bacteria and fungi are decomposers. They break down dead animals and plants, whose nutrients can then be used again to create new life.

Protective ozone

A blanket of gases many miles above Earth, called the ozone layer, stops dangerous rays from the Sun reaching the Earth. This protects all living things from harm.

Good for our health

When the natural system is working well, spending time in it can be really good for our physical and mental wellbeing.

Amazing atmosphere

Gases in the air, called atmosphere, allow the right amounts of heat to enter and leave Earth. If we put too much carbon dioxide into the atmosphere, the Earth will become too hot and lead to what is known as climate change.

Animal breathers

Animals breathe in oxygen and release carbon dioxide.

Incredible oceans

Tiny plants in the ocean take in carbon dioxide and give out oxygen. The ocean itself absorbs heat and spreads it around the planet.

The human problem

Our planet provides us with everything we need to survive, but we don't always treat it with kindness. Human actions are disrupting the Earth's perfect system and threatening life here. Here are some of the things we do that are harmful:

Damaging the ozone

Gases created by humans have damaged the ozone layer, meaning it can't protect us from the Sun as well.

Building concrete jungles

We lay concrete over green spaces so humans can live, work, and play there. Our towns and cities are built on areas that were once covered in plants and trees.

Only a small number of animals can survive in human cities.

Deforestation

We cut down trees to use their wood. We also clear areas of forest to make space for homes, roads, and mines. When wood is burned, the carbon it contains is released into the atmosphere.

Unkindness to others

We don't always treat other people with kindness, either. Sometimes they are treated badly because of the way they look, their gender, or the colour of their skin.

Burning fossil fuels

Fossil fuels such as gas, oil, and coal release energy when we burn them, which we use for electricity and transport. But burning them creates harmful carbon dioxide.

Disconnecting from nature

We are less connected to the natural world than we have ever been before. Many people go days or weeks without spending time in nature. It is hard to care about something if you don't know anything about it.

Producing waste

A lot of the waste we produce cannot be broken down by natural processes. Instead we collect it in huge piles of rubbish.

Polluting the ocean

Too much of the waste created by humans ends up in the ocean, where it can harm wildlife.

Sustainability

We often act as if the world's resources will never run out. We take and take, without giving the planet a chance to catch up. This way of acting is unsustainable, which means that it cannot carry on for a long time because eventually there will be no resources left.

Long-term living

It is possible to live in a way that uses up less resources. Living sustainably means living in a way that could carry on for a very long time, without causing any more damage to the planet.

If every person on Earth lived as unsustainably as the average person in the UK, we would need

THREE

planet Earths to support us all!

Indigenous lifestyles

Indigenous people often live in ways that are much more sustainable than the lifestyles other people are used to. They often have a strong connection to their environment and understand that they must treat it with kindness so that it will continue to provide for their children and grandchildren.

What can you do?

Consider the impact of every decision you make. Before buying something new, think about where it came from, how it was made and transported, and what will happen when you are finished with it. And ask whether you need to buy it at all! Often, living more simply is the best way to live a sustainable life.

Choose sustainable **energy**

This includes energy generated by wind, the Sun, and the sea.

Choose sustainable **travel**

Cycling, walking, and taking public transport when you can will help reduce your carbon footpint.

Use **water** sustainably

For example, turn off the water while you're brushing your teeth and take shorter showers.

Choose sustainable **food**

Eating less meat and more fruit and vegetables is better for the planet, and for your health, too!

15

The actions you take every day have

To save the planet, we need to educate ourselves.

important consequences for the planet.

The issues facing our planet are complex

Learn more about them by reading books, researching online, and watching documentaries. Experts and scientists have dedicated their lives to researching these issues. They can provide facts and figures to help you make your decisions.

Listen to different opinions

There are many ways of thinking about each problem. It is important to listen to lots of different opinions, even if you disagree.

Talk to the people affected

The people who are directly affected by an issue are the experts on how it impacts their lives and emotions – talk to them. They might tell you something you hadn't thought about before.

Be open-minded

This can help you to see the world in a more balanced way. Be prepared to change your mind, because your original way of thinking might not have been based on all of the facts.

climate change

Our planet is changing. The Earth is hotter than it was even a hundred years ago. This is mainly because of humans – our lifestyles produce dangerous gases, which mess with the Earth's perfect system.

Keeping warm

The surface of the Earth is heated by the Sun. Special gases in our atmosphere prevent some of this heat from leaving, keeping our planet at just the right temperature. They are known as greenhouse gases, and include carbon dioxide and methane. When the Earth's system is working properly, there is just the right amount of these gases in the atmosphere.

The human cause

But humans are adding more greenhouse gases to the atmosphere so the system is unbalanced.

- Trees store carbon dioxide. When we cut them down, the gas is released into the atmosphere.

- Burning fossil fuels for energy releases greenhouse gases.

- Waste that we have sent to landfill sites lets off greenhouse gases when it rots.

The effect

When there is extra gas in the atmosphere, more heat gets trapped and the Earth gets hotter. Even a small increase in temperature can have a big impact on our planet, and we are already seeing changes.

- Glaciers and sea ice are melting, which is causing sea levels to rise.

- Floods and droughts happen more often.

- Extreme weather events such as tornadoes, wildfires, and rain storms are more common.

- Greater levels of carbon dioxide in the ocean are dangerous for the plants and animals that live there.

switch it off

Imagine a life without electricity. It would be very different, wouldn't it? There would be no electric lights, no television, no iPads, and no phones. But do you know where electricity comes from? We get most of our electricity by burning fossil fuels.

Fossil fuels

Fossil fuels were formed around 300 million years ago from dead animals and plants. There are three different types: coal, oil, and natural gas. They are buried deep underground, so extracting them can be very harmful to the environment.

We burn fossil fuels to make electricity, to heat our homes, and to power cars, buses, trains, and planes. But burning them releases large amounts of carbon dioxide, a greenhouse gas. Supplies of fossil fuels won't last forever – they will eventually run out, so we call them non-renewable.

The renewable solution

There are other ways of making electricity that are renewable. This means they won't run out. For example:

Wind power, which is created when wind blows a turbine.

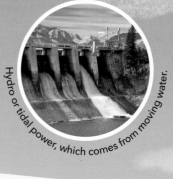

Hydro or tidal power, which comes from moving water.

Solar power, which comes from the Sun.

How to reduce your fossil fuel use

Here are some ideas:

- Walk or cycle instead of taking the car.
- Put on an extra layer of clothing instead of turning up the heating.
- Turn off lights and electronics when you are not using them.
- Use energy-saving lightbulbs.
- Talk to your grown-up about getting your energy from a renewable source.
- Use less plastic, as it is made from fossil fuels.
- Take shorter showers.

Plant a tree

Forests are one of nature's most wonderful creations. They provide homes and food for thousands of different animals, absorb harmful greenhouse gases, and even provide us with oxygen to breathe.

Super trees!

Trees are very important for keeping our planet running as it should.

- Trees release water from their leaves into the air, which later falls as rain.
- Tree roots anchor the soil, preventing it from being washed away.
- Trees provide shade for animals and plants.
- Fallen leaves provide the soil with nutrients.
- Trees take in carbon dioxide and give out oxygen.

Save our trees

But trees are cut down for many reasons: to graze cattle on the land, to use their wood for fuel or timber, to build mines, or to create cities and roads. Cutting down trees is really bad news for the planet.

Trees are good for you too!

Forests and woodlands are good for the soul. Connecting with the trees in your local area can be a great way to relax when you are feeling stressed.

Here are some tips for getting to know your local trees:

Make a bark rubbing.

Sit in the shade of a tree and draw or read.

Collect fallen fruits, nuts, or seeds.

If there are no trees in your local area, why not plant some? Pick a native species and do some research about what sort of conditions it likes before finding the perfect spot.

The Amazon Rainforest

The Amazon is the largest rainforest on Earth. It is home to 10 per cent of all known species of plants and animals, and more than 30 million people. But deforestation and climate change are causing the Amazon to disappear. If we don't make a change soon, a quarter of it will be lost by 2030.

Eat local meat

Rainforest land is cleared to graze cattle and grow soy beans to feed the cows and other livestock. You can support the Amazon by buying locally grown meat, which has not been grown on deforested land.

80%

of Amazon deforestation is to make space for cattle, that are grown for food.

Buy a rainforest

For your birthday, you could ask if your grown-up can buy you a patch of rainforest. This will protect it from damage by logging or mining.

Reuse paper

Paper is made from trees, so use it carefully. Write on both sides and fill all the blank spaces on each piece of paper before you throw it away, then recycle it when you are finished.

GO FSC

Look out for the FSC logo on your paper and wood products. It tells you that they have been made in a responsible way.

Protect its people

Many indigenous people live sustainably within the forest. They hunt forest animals to eat, take honey from forest bees, and grow crops in gardens. Their way of life is threatened by the destruction of the Amazon Rainforest.

People

Humans are very resourceful. They have managed to make homes all over the world. Sadly though, in some of these places, people are suffering because of human actions.

Indigenous living

The homes of people who have lived in places for thousands of years, called indigenous people, are at risk from issues such as poisonous chemicals polluting the rivers where they swim and fish, deforestation, and mining.

Education

For some children, learning how to care for the planet is something they are taught at school. But millions of children all over the world are not lucky enough to have access to a school. For them, learning how to treat the planet kindly is just one of many important lessons that they will miss.

Water

Billions of people don't have clean drinking water or a clean, private place to go to the toilet. In some places, water is polluted by human sewage. In others, water contains dangerous chemicals from processes such as dyeing clothes.

Poverty

The world has enough resources to keep everyone healthy and safe, but they are not shared out evenly. Nearly 690 million people are hungry, largely due to wars and climate change.

Equality

All people are equal, but they aren't always treated that way. Some people are treated worse because of the colour of their skin, their gender, or where they are from. This is wrong – our differences make us special.

War

In some areas, fighting and violence make it too dangerous for people to stay in their homes. These people must flee and search for somewhere safe to try and rebuild their lives. Sometimes they can never return to their homes.

conserve water

Water is very precious. All animals need clean drinking water to survive. Humans also use it for washing, cooking, creating new products, and much more. It is so important to not waste water, so that everybody has enough.

factories use lots of water:

- To dilute chemicals.
- To wash products.
- To cool machinery.

Less than 1% of Earth's water is available for drinking.

water pollution

Water can become polluted in many different ways. For example, this could be from leakages and spills from oil pipelines, chemicals dumped illegally by factories, fertilisers from farms, litter left by people on land, or people flushing the wrong things down the toilet.

water and people

Sadly, not everyone has access to clean water. Around the world, more than 2 billion people have to drink water polluted by human and animal poo. This can cause serious diseases such as cholera, dysentery, and polio. In some places, people walk many hours to collect clean water. What's more, 1 in 3 people do not have a private, clean toilet to use.

How can you save water?

Save up bathwater to water the plants and flush the toilet.

Use a water butt to collect rainwater.

Turn off the tap while you brush your teeth.

Run the dishwasher and washing machine on short and cold cycles.

Put a flush saver in your toilet.

Take short showers instead of baths.

How to make a flush saver

1. Put a few stones into an empty 1 litre plastic bottle, fill with water, and replace the lid.

2. Ask permission, then place the bottle carefully in the cistern of your toilet.

Fast fashion

In the last 50 years, the way we buy clothes has totally changed. Instead of getting clothes that are made to last, we are now encouraged to buy cheap new clothes every time there is a new trend.

Who makes our clothes?

Millions of children are employed by the fashion industry, to do everything from planting and harvesting cotton plants to making clothes. Many of them are not paid a fair wage.

Made to break

In the past, people would wear the same clothes season after season, repairing them when they broke. Most clothes bought on high streets now are not made as well – they often break easily and are difficult to repair.

What to buy

Try to pick good quality clothes made from natural materials, which can be repaired when they break and worn again for many years.

Nasty chemicals

Toxic chemicals are used to dye many of our clothes. These often leak into local waterways, poisoning the people and animals who drink water from them.

Getting rid of clothes

When your clothes no longer fit you, that doesn't have to be the end of their life.

- Swap them with your friends.
- Get creative - use the fabric in crafts or art projects.
- Recycle them - cut them up to make something new, such as cleaning cloths.
- Donate them to a charity shop - but only if they are still good quality!

Buying with kindness

We all buy more than we really need. One of the best things you can do for the planet is to buy less. When you do buy something, think about how to do it in a way that is kind to people, animals, and the environment.

Easy on the electronics

Minerals such as gold and copper are used to make electronic devices. They have to be extracted from the ground, which can be very damaging to the environment and dangerous for the people who do it. Do not replace your electronics unless you have to.

Limitless libraries

We are all familiar with the idea of taking a book out of the library, but did you know that you can borrow other things too? There are libraries for toys, libraries for clothes, libraries for electronics, and even libraries for musical instruments!

Every penny counts

Buy from companies that make things in a way that is kind to people and the planet. Your money will help them to continue making their products responsibly.

Look for labels

Keep your eyes peeled for labels that show an object has been produced in a responsible way. These could include:

- MSC (Marine Stewardship Council)
- FSC (Forest Stewardship Council)
- Fairtrade or WFTO (World Fair Trade Organisation)
- Rainforest Alliance
- Palm Oil Free
- Leaping Bunny

Beware cheap products

If a deal seems too good to be true, it probably is. Cheap items are often poor quality, or have been made in a way that treats people unfairly. Fairtrade labels tell you that the people who made the item were paid fairly.

Buy Secondhand

Good quality items can last for years and have many different homes. Buying secondhand things and looking after them so they can be passed on again is one of the best ways to prevent unnecessary waste.

The Rs

There are lots of ways we can help to tackle waste.
The most important thing we can do is not to buy too much in the first place. But for the things that we already have, there are lots of alternatives to putting them in the bin.

Recycle

Check with your local council which materials they can recycle. Some materials cannot be recycled in your household rubbish but you can take them to be collected from local recycling points.

Reuse

Ask how could you use it again? Use a tin can as a pencil holder or store small toys in an ice cream tub. Get a grown-up to help, though.

Watch for sharp edges!

Repair

Don't throw things away just because they are broken. Learn how to fix them or ask a grown-up for help.

Repurpose

With a bit of creative thinking, rubbish can be used in all sorts of projects. Plastic bottles can be made into musical instruments, bird feeders, or plant pots. What else can you think of?

Refuse

Next time you are offered something free, such as a pen, a badge, or a wristband, think about whether you really need it. How long will you use it for before throwing it away? What effect will it have on the planet?

Rot

Some rubbish, such as vegetable peelings, can be composted at home. Once it has rotted down, the compost can be used to grow plants.

Rehome

Pass on your old clothes to a younger sibling or someone in the year below you at school. Have a toy swap with your friends. Give good quality things to a charity shop so they can be sold on.

What a waste

When something is no longer useful to us, we throw it away. What does that really mean though? There is no such place as "away", but there are several places our waste can end up...

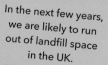

In the next few years, we are likely to run out of landfill space in the UK.

Incineration

In the UK, we are lucky that someone comes in a big truck to collect our rubbish. In many countries, waste is thrown out onto the

Landfill

Also known as rubbish heaps or dumps, landfills are enormous holes in the ground where waste is buried.

Recycling plant

Some rubbish can be recycled – broken down and turned into

streets, where it stays, polluting the water and causing disease. Some of our rubbish that is taken away is incinerated (burned), which can produce energy.

They release toxic liquids and gases, which are poisonous to animals and people. They also contribute to climate change.

something new. It takes less energy to recycle something than to create a brand new product.

Zero waste challenge

Is it possible to live your life without producing ANY rubbish? Some people do. This is called "zero waste" living and it means you try not to send anything you are finished with to landfill.

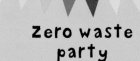

Zero waste party

Parties often create lots of waste, but it is possible to have a zero waste party!

- Ask for pre-loved gifts.

- Make a bubble wand out of sticks and string instead of having balloons.

- Use reusable plates, cups, and cutlery – or ask people to bring their own.

- Make your own crisps instead of buying lots of packets.

37

Plastic is not fantastic

Plastic, which is made from fossil fuels, is light, strong, and flexible. But it is not a natural material, so it has no place in the natural cycle. Once we have finished with it, the planet has no way of getting rid of it.

Straws

Plastic cutlery

450 years to break down.

What is plastic used for?

Lots of useful things are made from plastic, from medical equipment such as oxygen masks and hearing aids, to clothing such as fleeces and trainers.

Water bottles

Food packaging

Plastic disposal

A lot of our waste plastic cannot be recycled, so plastic items are thrown into landfill or burned. Plastic doesn't rot away – it just breaks down into smaller pieces, called microplastics. This process can take hundreds of years, meaning a lot of items hang around for a very long time:

Single-use plastic

Many plastic items are designed to be used once and then thrown away. We call these single-use plastics.

450 years to break down.

Nappies

20 years to break down.

Plastic bags

50 years to break down.

Plastic cups   Milk carton

Plastic swaps

Try to use less plastic by making some simple swaps:

- Use a bar of soap instead of a squeezy bottle of shower gel.

- Replace your plastic toothbrush with a bamboo one.

- Carry a reusable water bottle with you so you don't have to buy a single-use plastic bottle.

- Take a reusable cloth bag to the shops so you don't have to use plastic bags.

- Say no to straws!

Making plastics uses lots of energy and oil and adds to climate change. If plastics are not treated carefully when thrown away, they can harm people and wildlife.

Ocean plastic

About 9 million tonnes (9.9 million tons) of the plastic we throw away every year ends up in the sea. If we don't take action, by 2050 there will be 750 million tonnes (826 million tons) of plastic in the world's oceans.

How does it get there?

It's not just rubbish dropped on the beach that gets into the ocean. Plastics blow off landfill sites into the sea, rubbish is flushed down toilets so it enters the water system, and litter on the streets is washed into drains by rain. The equivalent of a rubbish truck full of plastic enters the ocean every minute.

Seabirds

Brightly coloured pieces of plastic, particularly those covered in food, are very attractive to seabirds, who will eat them. In the worst affected places, plastic can make up more than 90 per cent of the birds' diet.

Islands of plastic

Floating plastic collects on the surface of the water and forms huge islands in the middle of the ocean. The biggest of these islands, the Great Pacific Garbage Patch, contains nearly two trillion pieces of rubbish.

Fishing gear

Fishing nets and lines are also made of plastic. They are often left in the sea, where they create a huge problem for ocean animals, killing fish, turtles, birds, whales, and dolphins.

Microplastics

Pieces of plastic less than 5 mm (0.1 in) long are known as microplastics. Sea creatures eat these, thinking that they are food, which can kill them. We also sometimes eat microplastics – they can get into the bodies of fish which are then eaten by humans.

Oceans

Nearly three quarters of our planet is covered in water. Our vast oceans provide us with food, keep us warm, and release the oxygen we breathe. But, despite their size, there is a limit to how much we can take from our oceans.

Pollution

We pour all sorts of unpleasant things into the ocean, which can be damaging to ocean life. Sewage, oil, fertilisers, and rubbish all make their way into the sea.

We still have time to protect our remaining ocean animals but we must act now to save them before it is too late.

overfishing

Some types of fish have been caught in such huge numbers that they are now almost extinct. Not only is it devastating to lose species in this way, it also has a huge knock-on effect on the ocean food chain.

shark finning

Shark fins are highly prized in Asia, where they are used to make soup. Sadly, the fins are often cut off while the sharks are still alive, and the rest of their bodies are thrown back into the ocean.

Bycatch

Sometimes turtles, dolphins, and endangered fish become caught up in fishing nets and are injured or killed as a result. In pole and line fishing, only one fish is caught at a time, so it is a better way to catch fish.

captive animals

Most of the dolphins and whales you see in zoos, aquariums, and theme parks have been captured from the wild. These highly intelligent, sociable animals become very distressed as they are placed in tanks away from their families.

Bottom trawling

This is a destructive way to catch fish. Heavy nets are dragged along the ocean floor, destroying everything in their path. Other nets, such as purse seine nets, leave the ocean floor untouched instead.

Going, going, gone

In the 1730s, explorers discovered an incredible ocean mammal, which they called the Steller's sea cow. Within 30 years, it had been hunted to extinction. Protecting ocean life is so important.

Food

All animals need to eat.
There are lots of different
food options available to humans,
but the decisions we make about what to
eat and where to buy our food all have a
big effect on the environment. We need
to make these decisions carefully.

Large areas of
**Amazon
Rainforest**
are regularly destroyed
to rear cattle.

Meat and dairy

Raising animals for food uses a
lot of water. Animals need land
to graze on, and are often fed
with crops that have been grown
on deforested land. Cows also
belch out greenhouse gases.

Food miles

Before it reaches your plate, your food may already have been on quite a journey. Look out for the "country of origin" label on the packaging – this will tell you where it has travelled from to reach you.

Crops

In some places, forests are cut down to plant crops. This can mean that only one plant is grown for hundreds of miles. When this happens, the animals that lived in the forest become homeless, and there are no longer trees to capture greenhouse gases.

Cricket

Eat less meat

Beans, lentils, and pulses are good alternatives to meat. Eating insects is also becoming more popular. Insects are full of protein, are easy to grow, and need much less food and water than sheep and cows.

Food waste

In many countries, nearly a third of all food is wasted. Some food is destroyed or lost when it is being grown or transported, but most of it is wasted on our plates.

↖ Witchetty grub

Fat-bottomed ant

Love local

Supermarkets and the internet make shopping very easy, but shopping from these places is not always the kindest. Buying from local shops run by local people is a great way to support your neighbours and connect with your local community.

focus on farms

Farm shops make it possible to buy food directly from the place it is grown. This means that no fossil fuels are burned in order to transport it.

Blueberries from Chile have to travel more than **11,000 km (7,000 miles)** to reach your plate in the UK.

count the miles

If you counted up the miles your food has travelled, you would realise it has been on quite an adventure! But all that travel is bad for the planet. Try to make a meal with ingredients that have travelled less than 1,407 km (874 miles) – the length of the UK.

Good money sense

By spending money at a local shop, you put money back into your local area. In some places, you might even be able to get free fruit and vegetables in exchange for helping out.

Fantastically fresh

If food doesn't have to travel far, it is much fresher when you buy it. By buying from a farm shop, fruit and vegetables can come off the plant and be on your plate within a few hours!

Local adventure

There are plenty of other things you can do in your local area apart from shopping, such as going on holiday! For many people, the idea of going on holiday involves getting on a plane. But there are plenty of incredible places to visit in the UK too. Most of them can be reached without burning vast amounts of damaging fossil fuels.

Save the bees

Honeybees are famous for producing honey, but bees and other flying insects have another much more important job. They pollinate flowers, which helps our plants to produce babies, called seeds. Bees, wasps, beetles, moths, butterflies, and flies all pollinate our flowers. Many of our fruit and vegetables rely on insects to pollinate their plants.

What's happening to the bees?

Pollinating insects feed on nectar in flowers. If they have to travel too far between flowers, they don't have the energy to continue. By creating big concrete cities, building roads, and filling our gardens with patios, we make it much harder for pollinating insects to find their next meal. Pollinating insects are also killed by many of the chemicals we spray on our plants and crops.

How can we help?

Make a mini bee garden

Attract bees to your garden, balcony, or windowsill by planting a miniature garden, where bees can find something to eat and drink.

Include a bee-friendly plant, such as lavender, and a small dish full of water, with stones so the bees don't drown.

Bee-friendly plants

Plant wildflowers like honesty, buddleia, and hyssop in your garden or local wild space. Pick plants that flower at different times of year, so your fluttery visitors will always have a tasty snack.

Don't use chemicals

Chemical pesticides and fertilisers are as dangerous for helpful insects as they are for pests.

Don't mow the lawn

If you allow the grass to grow, it will flower. This will provide an important source of nectar for hungry insects.

Protect your patch

How well do you know the creatures living in your patch? You may not realise it, but there are lots of animals living right under your nose. Here are some ways you can get to know them better and keep them safe.

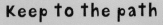

Keep to the path

Be careful not to trample on animals' homes when walking through grassy areas.

Feed the birds!

Leave out food and water for birds, wherever you live.

Join in with a wildlife survey

Scientists need to count animals such as butterflies and beetles. You can help! Find a survey online.

Explore local wild spaces

Visit them at different times of year and see which new plants and animals you can spot.

Leave out a log pile

Create a messy pile of logs and fallen leaves to create a warm hibernation spot for hedgehogs, frogs, and insects.

Keep your dog on a lead. It can scare **birds** that are nesting.

Stand up for your patch!

If your local wild patch is threatened, campaign to protect it.

Endangered Species

Human actions are threatening animal lives. Some animals are in such trouble that they may disappear from the Earth completely. They are known as endangered species. Pangolins are fascinating scaly creatures from Africa and Asia, but sadly they are in great danger.

It is likely that more than **one million** dead pangolins have been sold illegally since 2000.

chinese medicine

Pangolin scales are still used in traditional Chinese medicine by people suffering from many illnesses, but it is widely agreed that they don't work.

Meat

Pangolin meat is considered a delicacy in many parts of Asia.

Habitat loss

The forests that pangolins live in are threatened by deforestation.

Not my problem?

It's hard to believe that our actions affect animals far away, but they do! The forest habitats of pangolins are cut down to grow oil palm trees. Palm oil is used in many things from toothpaste to pizza. Sun bears, orangutans, and Sumatran rhinos are all threatened by planting oil palm trees.

what can I do?

Look out for products that are made without palm oil, or with sustainable palm oil, so you can make sure that your lifestyle does not support the destruction of pangolin homes.

Slow down

Thinking about the challenges facing our planet can be overwhelming. If it gets too much, take time to slow down and appreciate the good things around you. Spending time in nature is a great way to unwind.

Feel the magic

Incredible things happen in nature every single day. Experience one of many daily miracles – look at the stars, watch the sun rise or set, or listen to the birds singing in the dawn chorus.

Get active

Take a refreshing dip in a river, lake, or the sea. Go for a walk, run, or cycle outside in the fresh air.

Get creative

Collect natural materials and embark
on some nature-themed crafts.
Or try sketching a landscape or
painting an animal or plant.

Be quiet

Reading a book under a
tree is very relaxing. Take a
moment to sit, surrounded
by nature, and do nothing.

Disconnect

Turn off your devices
and connect with
nature instead.

Ground yourself in your senses

Name three things you can smell,
three things you can hear,

three things you
can see, and three
things you can feel.

Have your say

If you think something is wrong or unfair, don't be a bystander. Stand up for what you believe and make your voice heard.

Get political

To make big changes, we need the help of the government and MPs. You can influence their actions by voting for the parties that treat the planet kindly and writing to your local MP about issues that are important to you.

Make every word count

Follow these guidelines to help your letter make the biggest possible impact:

- Be polite.

- Use facts and evidence.

- Explain why the issue matters so much to you personally.

- Don't just list the problems – suggest solutions too.

- Include a return address.

- If you don't get the response you were hoping for, try again.

Spread the word

Take every opportunity to tell people about the issues facing our planet. Give an assembly at school, put up posters in your local area, and pester your grown-ups to make planet-friendly decisions.

Be an ally

For some people, life is made easier by things they can't control, such as where they live or the colour of their skin. These advantages are called privilege. If we are lucky enough to benefit from privilege, it is important that we use our position to help people, animals, and environments that do not benefit from it.

Actions speak louder than words

Live your life in a way that is respectful of the planet. If your friends and family see you making changes to your lifestyle then they may follow your example.

Heal the Earth

Even though we have damaged it, our planet is very resilient. If we stop treating it badly and give it time and space to recover, the Earth can heal. There are many ways to live in a way that is less damaging to the planet.

car-free cities

Many cities now have car-free centres where people can walk and cycle safely. This vastly improves the air quality and reduces the city's carbon footprint.

Grey to green

We need more plants, but people still need places to live and work. It is amazing how much greenery can be squeezed into a grey city when you get creative!

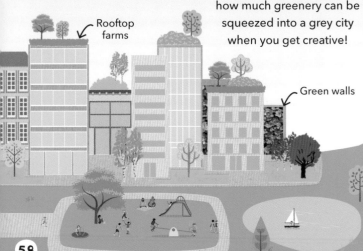

Rooftop farms

Green walls

Wild again

In 1986, the area around Chernobyl in Ukraine was evacuated because of a nuclear disaster. Now, although humans can't live there, the area has become a haven for wildlife.

Energy-efficient buildings

Clever planning and building can help us to create houses, shops, and offices that take very little energy to run.

Wind turbines

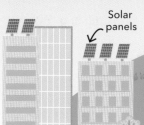

Solar panels

Green energy

Our fossil fuels will soon run out. We need to find different ways to power our cities, such as using energy from the sun or wind.

Protect and provide

If we protect the planet in the right way, it can provide for us. For example, with the right protection, the amount of wildlife in Cabo Pulmo marine reserve in Mexico increased four times in just 10 years.

Building for the future

We are all equal

Treat each and every person with kindness.
We do not all look, act, or sound the same,
but we are all equal and all of our opinions
are important. By working together and valuing
everyone equally, we can achieve great things.

Look after YOU

You have the power to change the world, but
protecting a whole planet can take up a lot of
time and energy. Make sure you look after
yourself by eating heathily, sleeping lots, and
relaxing. Grown-ups are always there to help
you if you are struggling to do any of these things.

Small things make a big difference

No act of kindness is wasted. If we all do one thing each day that is kind to people, animals, and the environment, the world will quickly become a better place.

You won't be small forever

Just as tiny acorns grow into huge oak trees with an important role to play in the forest, you too will grow into an old and wise person with an important role to play in the world. Never forget the importance of kindness, and use your wisdom and strength to support those that are less fortunate than you.

Without nature we have nothing

Without healthy trees and oceans, humans cannot exist. Our own survival depends on us starting to make decisions that put the health of the planet first. Lots of damage has already been done and the planet needs time to heal, but there is still time to save it. We have the knowledge, we have the power, but we must act **NOW**.

That's it!

You've learned:

what the problems are,
why we need to make a change, and
how you can make a difference.

So what are you waiting for?
Off you go, incredible human.

It's time to protect the planet.

Glossary

atmosphere
Layer of gases that surrounds a planet

carbon footprint
The amount of greenhouse gases (including carbon dioxide and methane) that our lifestyle creates

climate change
Change in temperature and weather across the Earth that can be natural or caused by human activity

deforestation
Cutting down trees and destroying forests

endangered
When an animal or plant species is low in number and could become extinct

fertiliser
A substance added to soil or land to help plants to grow

fossil fuel
A fuel made from animals and plants that died millions of years ago, such as coal, oil, and natural gas

greenhouse gas
A gas in the Earth's atmosphere that traps heat, like a greenhouse, and warms the planet

indigenous person
Someone who is part of a community that has lived in a place for a long time, and hasn't moved there from somewhere else

landfill
A place where rubbish is buried in the ground

microplastics
Very small pieces of plastic that pollute the environment

MP

Stands for Member of Parliament: a person who has been elected to the parliament of a country

nutrients

Types of food that animals and plants need to survive

overfishing

Catching too many fish in an area of water, so that there are not many fish left there

ozone layer

An area in the Earth's atmosphere that protects the surface from the Sun's harmful rays

pollution

Something harmful that gets into the air, a water source, or the soil

privilege

When a person's life is made easier by something they can't control, such as the colour of their skin or where they are from

renewable

A type of fuel or energy that will not run out, such as wind, or of which can be made or grown, such as trees

sustainable

Use of materials in such a way that they will not run out or become too hard to find

zero waste

When nothing is sent to landfill, and anything finished with is reused or recycled

Index

A, B

activism 56-57
Amazon Rainforest 24-25
animals 11, 40-43, 50-53, 59
atmosphere 11, 13, 18-19
bees 48-49

C, D

carbon dioxide 10, 11, 13, 18, 19, 20, 22
carbon footprint 19
carbon stores 11
cattle 24, 44
charity shops 31, 35
chemicals, toxic 29, 31
Chinese medicine 53
cities 12, 58-59
climate change 11, 18-19, 24, 27, 37
clothing 30-31
compost 35
conservation 28-29, 59
crops 45
decomposers 10
deforestation 13, 18, 22, 24, 53
droughts 19

E

Earth system 10-11
education 16-17, 26
electricity 13, 20-21
electronic devices 32
endangered species 52-53
energy 15, 20-21, 59
equality 27, 60
extinctions 43, 53
extreme weather 19

F

Fairtrade labels 33
farm shops 46, 47
fashion industry 30-31
fertilisers 28, 42, 49
fires 19
fishing 41, 43
floods 19
flush savers 29
food 15, 44-47
food miles 45, 46
forests 22-23
fossil fuels 11, 13, 18, 20-21, 38, 47
FSC logo 25, 33

G, H

Great Pacific Garbage Patch 41
green energy 59
greenhouse gases 18, 19, 20, 22, 39
habitat loss 53
holidays 47
human impact 7, 12-13, 18, 26-27
hydro power 21

I, K

incineration 36-37
indigenous peoples 14, 25, 26
information 16-17
kindness 9, 13, 32-33, 60, 61

L, M

labels 33
landfill 19, 36-37
libraries 32
lifestyle 14, 18, 19, 57, 60
meat 24, 44-45, 53
microplastics 41

N, O

natural resources 14, 27
nature 13, 22, 54-55, 61
oceans 11, 13, 40-43, 61
oxygen 10, 11, 22, 42
ozone layer 11, 12, 18

P

palm oil 53
pangolins 52-53
paper 25
plastics 38-41
politics 56
pollination 48
pollution 13, 28, 29, 31, 42
poverty 27

R

reusing 35
recycling 10, 31, 34
recycling plants 36-37
renewable energy 21
repairing 30, 35
repurposing 35

S

sea levels, rising 19
seabirds 40
secondhand products 33
senses 55
shopping 46-47
single-use plastics 39
solar power 21
Sun 11, 12, 15, 18, 21, 54
sustainability 14-15

T

teamwork 8
temperatures 10, 11, 18, 19
tidal power 21
transport 15, 20, 58
trees 10, 18, 22-23, 61

W, Z

war 27
waste 13, 19, 36-37, 45
water 15, 27, 28-29, 31
wind power 21
zero waste 37

Acknowledgments

DK would like to thank Caroline Twomey for proofreading and Helen Peters for the index.

The publisher would like to thank the following for their kind permission to reproduce their photographs:

(Key: a-above; b-below/bottom; c-centre; f-far; l-left; r-right; t-top)

123RF.com: Eric Isselee / isselee 44clb, Olga Khoroshunova 28-29, peterwaters 48-49 (x4), Aleksey Poprugin 40-41 (x3), Roman Samokhin 40-41c (x2), sergemi 69cb (Christmas tree worms), smokhov 23bc, Dennis van de Water 24-25, Wavebreak Media Ltd 34crb, Svetlana Yefimkina 55cra (Leaves x2); **Alamy Stock Photo:** Design Pics Inc / Axiom / David Kirkland 14bl, F1online digitale Bildagentur GmbH / Tobias Friedrich 68bc, imageBROKER / SeaTops 69crb, Oksana Maksymova 69cra (Blotcheye Soldierfish), Luiz Puntel / Reef and Aquarium Photography 68br, WaterFrame_fur 68bl; **Dorling Kindersley:** Holts Gems 69cra, Natural History Museum, London 69clb, Linda Pitkin 69ca, Linda Pitkin 69crb (Sea strawberry), Quinn Glass, Britvic, Fentimans 40-41c (x3); **Dreamstime.com:** Ivan Aleksandrov 30bl, Alle 48cl, Alle 48cr, Artjazz 21cr, BY 38cb, 41 (x2), Sergiy Bykhunenko / Sbworld4 49 (Wood x6), 51br (Wood x2), Brett Critchley 45c, Ethan Daniels 69cr, Dream69 69cb, 69fcra, Ilka-erika Szasz-fabian 26b, Inbevel 27b, Eric Isselee 51cl, Viktoriia Khyzhniak 32br, Victor Koldunov 42bl, Daisuke Kurashima 68-69 (Blue banded snapper x6), Halim Lotososerdtsev 45crb, Manaemedia 32cl, Dimitar Marinov / Oorka 21tr, Minaret2010 57c, Matee Nuserm 51cra, Orlandin 68cra, 69fcr, Orlandin 68-69 (Spotted garden-eel x3), Pixelife 23crb, Pklimenko 12-13ca, Rawpixelimages 56-57 (Sticky x3), Rdiachkin 36-37t, Robwilson39 36cl, Alfio Scisetti / Scisettialfio 38cr, 40cra, 40clb, Alexander Shalamov / Alexshalamov 42cr, 69tr, Mykola Sirenko 36-37b, smikeymikey1 10br, Rechitan Sorin / Rechitansorin 28br, Anton Starikov 38cra, Toa555 27tl, Denis Trofimov 49cr, 49bc, Vchalup 36-37c, David Pereiras Villagra 41crb, Vvoevale 34-35bc (leaves), Tom Wang 31bc, Whitcomberd 69bl; **Fotolia:** Eric Isselee 25br; **Getty Images / iStock:** Androsov 21ca, ivanastar 12bl, marrio31 68cla, Gilles_Paire 30clb, Peter_Horvath 69clb (Angelfish), ptewort 15crb, stellalevi 8-9, 10-11, 16-17, 22-23, 46-47, t_kimura 34-35bc, tunart 59tl, yotrak 26t; **naturepl.com:** Suzi Eszterhas 52-53; **Photolibrary:** Photodisc / White 42cra; **PunchStock:** Westend61 / Rainer Dittrich 44tr

All other images © Dorling Kindersley
For further information see: www.dkimages.com

Coral reefs

Coral reefs are brightly coloured and bursting with life. They can be found in warm, tropical waters with lots of light. Reefs are very delicate environments, which are easily damaged by changing temperatures and pollution.

Copperband butterfly fish

Staghorn coral

Barracuda

Ribboned sweetlips

What is coral?

Corals are not plants. Each coral structure is made up of millions of tiny animals called polyps, which are related to jellyfish and sea anemones.

Bluestripe snapper

Giant clam

Crown-of-thorns starfish

Lettuce coral

Leaf plate montipora

Coral reefs are found in less than 1 per cent of the ocean, but are home to 25 per cent of ocean plant and animal species.

Hawksbill turtle

Bumphead parrotfish

Blotcheye soldierfish

Hard or soft?
Hard corals have rock-like skeletons and form the structure of the reef. Soft corals do not have these skeletons and look more like plants.

Walking shark

Eating coral
Adult corals are eaten by fish, worms, and sea stars.

Christmas tree worm

Red whip coral

Bicolour angelfish

Pygmy seahorse

Sea fan

Garden eel

Earth's Incredible OCEANS

Learn more about oceans with a brand new DK book by Jess French!

Enter the incredible world of oceans – swim with jellyfish, discover the busy life of a seagrass meadow, and fence with narwhals.

More titles from Jess French

There's so much more to discover about the world around you. Find out more here:

The Book of Brilliant Bugs

In the world of bugs, anything is possible. See fireflies dance, spiders spin, and marvel at the magical metamorphosis of a moth. You'll never look at bugs in the same way again...

What a Waste

Almost everything we do creates some sort of waste. Find out where it goes, how it is affecting the Earth, and how you can get involved to help make our beautiful planet a better place to live.

DK For the curious

www.dk.com

On your bookmarks, get set, read!

W ell hello there! We are

O verjoyed that you have joined our celebration of

R eading books and sharing stories, because we

L ove bringing books to you.

D id you know, we are a charity dedicated to celebrating the

B rilliance of reading for pleasure for everyone, everywhere?

O ur mission is to help you discover brand new stories and

O pen your mind to exciting worlds and characters, from

K ings and queens to wizards and pirates to animals and adventurers and so many more. We couldn't

D o it without all the amazing authors and illustrators, booksellers and bookshops, publishers, schools and libraries out there –

A nd most importantly, we couldn't do it all without . . .

You!

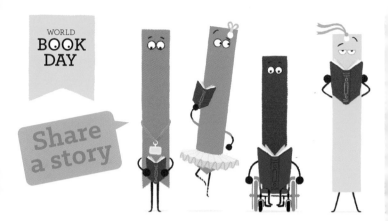

WORLD BOOK DAY

Share a story

From breakfast to bedtime, there's always time to discover and share stories together. You can . . .

1 Take a trip to your local bookshop

Brimming with brilliant books and helpful booksellers to share awesome reading recommendations, you can also enjoy booky events with your favourite authors and illustrators.

Find your local bookshop:
booksellers.org.uk/bookshopsearch

2 Join your local library

That wonderful place where the hugest selection of books you could ever want to read awaits – and you can borrow them for FREE! Plus expert advice and fantastic free family reading events.

Find your local library:
gov.uk/local-library-services/

3 Check out the World Book Day website

Looking for reading tips, advice and inspiration? There is so much to discover at **worldbookday.com**, packed with fun activities, audiobooks, videos, competitions and all the latest book news galore.

JESS FRENCH

PROTECT THE PLANET

Illustrated by
ALEESHA NANDHRA

This book belongs to:

- -

This World Book Day 2021 book is a gift
from your local bookseller and DK
#ShareAStory

Author Jess French
Illustrator Aleesha Nandhra

Editor Sophie Parkes
Project Art Editor Charlotte Bull
Designers Elle Ward, Charlotte Milner
Managing Editor Penny Smith
Managing Art Editor Mabel Chan
Production Editor Rob Dunn
Production Controller Ena Matagic
Jacket Designer Charlotte Bull
Jacket Illustrator Aleesha Nandhra
Jacket Editor Sophie Parkes
Art Director Helen Senior
Publishing Director Sarah Larter

Consultant Stephen Burnley

First published in Great Britain in 2021
by Dorling Kindersley Limited
DK, One Embassy Gardens,
8 Viaduct Gardens,
London, SW11 7BW

Imported into the EEA by
Dorling Kindersley Verlag GmbH.
Arnulfstr. 124, 80636 Munich, Germany

Copyright © 2021
Dorling Kindersley Limited
A Penguin Random House Company
10 9 8 7 6 5 4 3 2 1
001-323573-Feb/2021

A CIP catalogue record for this book
is available from the British Library.
ISBN: 978-0-2415-0204-4

Printed and bound in the UK

For the curious
www.dk.com

	MIX
FSC www.fsc.org	Paper from responsible sources **FSC™ C018179**

This book was made with
Forest Stewardship Council ™
certified paper – one small step in DK's
commitment to a sustainable future.

For more information go to
www.dk.com/our-green-pledge